Essential Viewpoints

The Welfare Debate

Essential Viewpoints

The Welfare Debate

BY KEKLA MAGOON

Content Consultant
Joe Barnett
Director of Publications
National Center for Policy Analysis

ABDO
Publishing Company

CREDITS

Published by ABDO Publishing Company, 8000 West 78th Street, Edina, Minnesota 55439.

Printed in the United States.

Editor: Paula Lewis
Copy Editor: Patricia Stockland
Interior Design and Production: Ryan Haugen
Cover Design: Becky Daum

Library of Congress Cataloging-in-Publication Data
Magoon, Kekla.
The welfare debate / by Kekla Magoon.
p. cm. — (Essential viewpoints)
Includes bibliographical references and index.
ISBN 978-1-60453-114-5
1. Public welfare—United States—Juvenile literature. I. Title.

HV95.M2625 2009
361.60973—dc22

2008011898

TABLE OF CONTENTS

Chapter 1

In 2005, this 33-year-old Michigan mother received $290 a month in food stamps to supplement her income.

Why Welfare?

Welfare is one of the most debated topics in U.S politics. Hundreds of billions of dollars are spent on U.S. welfare programs each year. The 2006 U.S. Census reported that more than 36.5 million citizens lived in poverty, and the number appears to be increasing. While there is a general agreement that welfare programs need reform, few people agree on what changes are needed. The welfare debate centers on one important question: what exactly should the government do to help its poorest citizens?

What Is Welfare?

Welfare is a very broad term. Generally, the word "welfare" describes the many programs and services that the government offers to support citizens who are poor. The most basic type of welfare is money that the government gives to people in need. This direct financial support is what people often think of first as welfare. When a poor family receives welfare money, they decide how to spend it. They might use it to pay for groceries, clothes, or rent. Families who receive welfare money would not be able to afford these necessary expenses without help.

Poverty in the United States

The official U.S. poverty rate in 2006 was 12.3 percent. That represents 36.5 million people, including 7.7 million families.

Money is not the only type of welfare that the government provides. Instead of allowing families to decide how the welfare money is spent, the government sometimes provides vouchers for important expenses such as food or housing. A voucher will pay for only one type of expense. Food stamps are a type of voucher. A family that receives food stamps can choose what kind of food to buy, but they cannot choose to pay rent or buy items such as clothes, tobacco, or alcohol with the food stamps. The government

Determining the Poverty Threshold

Determining the poverty threshold for individuals and families is a complex process. Each year, the U.S. Census Bureau releases estimates on how much it costs for households with varying numbers of family members to live in the United States. A family's poverty threshold depends on how its income compares to that number. Each family may have a different poverty threshold, depending on how much income they have and how many family members live together in one household. For example, in 2007, a family of four earning less than $20,650 per year was living in poverty.

There is debate about the best way to measure poverty. Some people think government assistance funds, such as housing vouchers and food stamps, should be included as part of each family's income. That way, some families who receive those services would appear to be above the poverty level. It would then seem that there are fewer poor people in the country. Other people think government assistance should not be included with a family's income. Welfare supporters, in particular, worry that those welfare programs might be cut once it appears that fewer people are poor. They fear that a new cycle of poverty would soon begin.

sometimes offers housing vouchers for families who cannot afford to pay rent.

Today, welfare is about more than just helping poor people pay for the things they need to live. Lawmakers have determined that the government should help struggling families get out of poverty. The government provides job-training programs and individual counseling to help people learn the skills needed to be hired and succeed at work. These programs also have become part of the welfare debate. Should welfare money be spent as direct payments to families, as vouchers, or for programs to help people become employed?

Welfare Programs

Examples of government assistance programs include:

- Food stamps: families receive coupons to pay for grocery items
- Low Income Home Energy Assistance Program: pays for heating and electricity for families in need
- National School Lunch Program: gives free or reduced-cost lunches to students
- Temporary Assistance for Needy Families (TANF): federal funds granted to states to provide families with job training and money to support basic needs for a short period of time

Welfare Families

For poor families, life can be a daily struggle. Food, clothing, housing, and heat are not guaranteed for people living in poverty. Poverty is a term used to describe families whose income is too low for them to live on. The amount of income a family needs to survive is determined by many factors, such as the cost of rent, the cost of food, and the number of people in the family. These factors change over time and affect the poverty threshold. In 2006, the U.S. population was approximately 299.4 million people. That year, of the 36.5 million people living below the poverty threshold, approximately 12.8 million were children.

People fall into poverty for many reasons. Unemployment is one reason, but many people living in poverty have jobs that simply do not pay enough to meet their basic needs. A lack of education and training can prevent people from getting and keeping better-paying jobs. Raising children costs money. Poor health that makes it difficult to work or an illness that is costly to treat can cause a family to fall into poverty. Many low-wage workers with families simply cannot afford all the expenses, no matter how many hours they work. For children, living in poverty depends entirely on their parents' income. Since children have no control over family earnings, many welfare laws are designed to help protect children from hunger, homelessness, and suffering.

This single mother with three children was on welfare. She took classes to become a police officer and support her family without welfare aid.

Challenge to Lawmakers

Welfare programs are funded through the government. Citizens pay taxes to the government based on their incomes. People with higher incomes pay more taxes than people with lower incomes. Congress and the president of the United States are responsible for determining how much tax money to collect to pay for welfare. They also must decide how that welfare money will be spent.

Many politicians and lawmakers agree that it is important for the government to help poor families. What they do not agree about is the best way to do it. Some people believe that the main problem is low incomes. They want to see more welfare money distributed. Although welfare recipients need financial help, other people believe that they might not spend that money properly. They want to see more food stamps and voucher programs for housing to ensure the money is well spent. Still others believe that getting poor people into better jobs will reduce poverty. They want to see the government offer job training, career counseling, and money-management classes.

And there are those who believe that giving money is not the answer at all. They want to end welfare programs and return the money to the taxpayers. They believe that, with lower taxes, businesses will be able to offer higher wages to workers, thus helping workers out of poverty.

Welfare opponents argue that giving money means giving a handout to people who have not earned it. They say people need to get jobs and make their own way. They worry that people will take advantage of the system by collecting a welfare check and not looking for work. These opponents believe if less welfare money is available, poor people will have more incentive to get jobs to help themselves.

Those who favor welfare argue that it is not behavior but circumstance that puts people in poverty. They believe that the government must step in to support struggling people, and people who can work will make an effort to do so. The more welfare money that is available will make it easier for poor people to get back on their feet.

"The welfare reform debate has remained contentious and emotional, because it touches the most sensitive of societal issues: work, family . . . personal responsibility, and community integrity. Welfare reform [asks] fundamental questions about quality of life and how to allocate personal and public responsibilities. . . . We even debate the fundamental goals of reform—to save money or save people; to reduce poverty or minimize welfare dependency?"[1]

—*Thomas Corbett, Assistant Professor, School of Social Work, University of Wisconsin*

Scholars, economists, politicians, and citizens have studied welfare strategies for decades. Strong arguments exist to defend these strategies. Equally strong arguments exist to reject them. Who must make these important decisions? Why is this a difficult issue to solve?

The welfare debate continues because these perspectives are so different. It is difficult to determine the best approach. It has taken decades for U.S. society to sort through these ideas, and the country still is debating the welfare issue. The problem has not been solved; dealing with poverty is complex. Plus, welfare policies cannot be considered alone. Laws regarding welfare are strongly affected by laws about health care, education, employment, and housing. Lawmakers must consider all these factors when legislating what is best for welfare. What is the government's responsibility to its poorest citizens? Who is talking about welfare and what are they saying? How can citizens contribute to the welfare debate?

In 2004, this psychiatric aid made $8.45 an hour. She relied on welfare that included food stamps for her family.

Chapter 2

In late 2007, Governor Rendell announced that Pennsylvania would receive more than $3 million for managing the food stamp program.

Key Players in the Welfare Debate

There are many opinions about welfare. Who are the major voices in the debate? Lawmakers, businesses, service organizations, government agencies, and citizens are all involved in the conversation. Many groups lobby for different approaches to reform. Each one plays a role in shaping welfare policies.

Lawmakers

The president and Congress are responsible for creating laws that control welfare policies for the entire country. Large-scale welfare programs such as Temporary Assistance for Needy Families (TANF), National School Lunch Program, and Social Security are federal programs. Federal laws that promote economic growth and equal opportunities, such as the Civil Rights Act and the Economic Opportunity Act, benefit every citizen.

Mayors, governors, and state legislators make decisions about how to use federal welfare funds. State governments must develop the local programs that will turn the welfare ideas into help for real people. It is a big responsibility. Local governments must communicate with the federal government and inform it about what is going on in their communities. This helps Congress pass laws that are based on real needs. This is a difficult

Minimum Wage

The federal minimum wage is the smallest amount of money a worker can be paid for an hour of work. In January 2007, Congress voted to raise the federal minimum wage from $5.15 to $7.25 per hour. The increase would occur in increments over a two-year period.

process involving conversations, ideas, statistics, and debate. Most discussions end in some form of compromise.

Lobbyists

Lobbyists are sometimes accused of using unethical tactics to convince elected officials to vote a certain way. Congress imposed new ethics reforms and rules in 2007. These rules restrict the amount of money and the value of gifts or services lobbyists can give to a member of Congress. It would be unfair for anyone to be able to buy an elected official's vote. A system based on democracy means everyone, rich or poor, should have an equal voice in talking to elected officials.

Lobbyists

Lobbyists are people hired by private companies or groups to influence how elected officials vote. For instance, when Congress was considering raising the minimum wage, some companies hired lobbyists to go to Washington DC. The lobbyists tried to convince members of Congress that raising the minimum wage would be bad for businesses. Private organizations that work with welfare recipients also sent lobbyists to Washington DC. Those lobbyists tried to convince members of Congress that raising the minimum wage would help poor families.

Organizations

Liberal, conservative, and nonpartisan groups all study welfare. Different organizations examine the issue from different angles. Some compile extensive statistics that other people can use. Others write essays and articles defending ideas for their side of the debate. Others study the individuals who benefit from welfare and those who may be hurt by it. Still others analyze the political processes that are involved in creating legislation.

All the groups ask important questions to help them make decisions. Does welfare impact work? How does welfare affect children? How does it connect with health care, education,

Marches on Washington

Motivated citizens sometimes make their opinions public. Washington DC, as the nation's capital, is often selected as the site for a demonstration. Marches have included:

- March 3, 1913, Women's Suffrage March: Women united to call for voting rights for women.
- August 28, 1963, March on Washington for Jobs and Freedom: People called for an end to segregation and workplace discrimination.
- April 17, 1965, March Against the Vietnam War: Students for a Democratic Society organized the first national protests against the war.
- January 22, 1974, March for Life: Pro-life activists protested the Supreme Court's *Roe v. Wade* decision that legalized women's right to choose abortion. This march has been held every year since 1974.
- February 5, 1979, Tractorcade: Family farmers rode tractors into Washington DC to protest farm policies.
- October 12, 1979, National March on Washington for Lesbian and Gay Rights: People supported equal rights for gays and lesbians.
- October 16, 1995, Million Man March: African-American men promoted voter registration and reenergized important issues for African-American communities.

and immigration? Is welfare good or bad for the economy? Who should manage welfare and what are its goals? Is it succeeding?

Many groups study the issues. These groups include: the Heritage Foundation, a conservative policy group; the Roosevelt Institute, a nonpartisan student think tank in New York; the Institute for Research on Poverty; the National Poverty Center; and the National Center for Children in Poverty.

Citizens

Any citizen can take part in the welfare debate. Citizens often participate by working with organizations that deal with welfare programs. They also can contact their elected officials to share their thoughts about welfare. Elected officials have a responsibility to create the kinds of government programs that their constituents want.

Activists outside the nation's capitol protested proposed cuts to social welfare programs.

Chapter 3

In the 1600s, New England Puritans discussed ways to help the poor.

Origins of Welfare in the United States

In any society, there are bound to be some people who are very wealthy, some people who are very poor, and a lot of people who fall somewhere in between. This has always been the case in the United States, but governments, communities, and individuals have always tried to help people in need.

Welfare in Early America

Most of the American colonies were made up of small towns and villages. These towns based their government on the laws of England, from which many of the colonists had come. In England, social classes remained quite constant. People who were born rich stayed rich, people who were born poor stayed poor. Churches and private donations helped the poor. People believed that social classes would always exist and that rich people should help the less fortunate.

In the colonies, small communities shared the burden of caring for the poorest families. Neighbors looked out for each other by making sure everyone had enough wood to burn, food to eat, and other survival essentials. Town leaders often allowed poor families to collect firewood and plant vegetable gardens on public property. Beggars who went door-to-door were rarely turned away empty-handed.

This worked well at the time. Towns grew, and larger communities meant more people, especially more poor people, living closer together. The community-based style of welfare also changed. It became more difficult for individuals to do enough to help each other.

Capitalism and Democracy

When the United States became an independent, democratic nation, everything changed. Democracy changed the way people viewed social class. It erased the idea that the rich must stay rich and the poor must stay poor. It gave all citizens a voice in government and a chance to improve their positions.

The U.S. economic system of capitalism meant that all people had the opportunity to make money, if they worked to earn it. Anyone could become rich in this new nation. Many people emigrated from Europe and other places around the world to be part of the American dream. Many immigrants arrived with very little money and limited job skills. They

Poor Laws

The earliest welfare practices in the colonies were based on British poor laws. During the reign of Queen Elizabeth I (1558–1603), a series of laws were passed to instruct people on how to deal with the poor. The laws divided the poor into three categories: people who were willing but unable to work, people who were able but unwilling to work, and people who were too old or too young to work.

In 1601, Britain's Poor Law Act allowed two different types of relief for the poor. Indoor relief included housing beggars in the poorhouse, orphans in orphanages, and sick people in hospitals. Outdoor relief included giving people money, food, supplies, or clothing to help them survive in their own homes. This act also imposed the first community tax to be used for poor relief.

had made the difficult journey hoping that, with hard work, their lives would work out for the best.

Urban versus Rural

During the nineteenth century, U.S. cities grew larger as immigrants poured in. Most arrived with very little money. They worked hard to capture the American dream and become rich. Some succeeded, but many struggled just to survive. The cities became crowded with poor people. The country faced a new problem: urban poverty. What was to be done to help the cities' poor?

At the same time, the country was expanding westward. Explorers and settlers ventured out across the plains and mountains. Some were trying to escape the cities. Others wanted adventure or a different kind of life. Those who moved to the West became farmers or ranchers and tended large areas of land. People had more space, but some still struggled to make ends meet. There were many differences between the urban environment and the rural environment. But there were poor people in both environments.

With the end of the U.S. Civil War in 1865, African Americans who had been slaves throughout the South became free. Many freed slaves moved to the North to cities such as Chicago, New York, Philadelphia, and Washington DC. Others became farmers or sharecroppers and tended land in the South and West. Freed slaves had little or no money. This added to the number of poor people in the country who needed to find work.

Forty Acres and a Mule

At the end of the Civil War, General William Tecumseh Sherman marched his Union Army troops across Georgia to the sea. The war was over and the Union had won. Newly freed slaves joined Sherman's troops. In January 1865, Sherman issued a Special Field Order. He declared that a 400,000-acre (161,874-ha) section of the southeastern United States should be reserved so that freed slaves could own 40-acre (16-ha) pieces of property. Sherman also allowed extra mules and horses that were no longer needed for the war effort to be given to the new landowners. A government agency called the Freedmen's Bureau was created to oversee the land distribution. Approximately 40,000 freed slaves lived in the area within a few months of Sherman's order. The government was using its resources to offer poor families an opportunity that otherwise was far out of reach.

About a year later, Congress voted to end the Freedmen's Bureau. The land was taken back from the African-American families and returned to Caucasian landowners. This was devastating to the new landowners. Since former slaves had not earned wages working on the plantations, they could not afford to buy the land. They were forced to leave.

Organized Aid

Especially in cities, poverty became a very significant problem during the late nineteenth century. Large groups of very poor people lived close together in harsh conditions, creating communities plagued with illness, crime, and sorrow. This was a time before electricity, running water, and sewer systems. The streets were filthy. The slum buildings, where poor people lived, stank and were infested with bugs and rodents. And unlike rural areas, there was little open space to create a garden.

Community and religious groups took pity on the poor. They opened soup kitchens and operated programs to help struggling people. Cities created poorhouses to shelter the most destitute people. Citizens and lawmakers became involved in serious debates on public welfare policies.

But how much should the government be responsible for taking care of the poor? Some people still believed that poverty was a result of circumstances. Others blamed laziness and failure. They worried that giving money to the poor would discourage people from working.

While lawmakers tried to figure out what to do about poverty, poor people suffered. The rich and middle-class people living in nearby neighborhoods became disturbed by the slums. They began to look down on poor people, and some even feared them.

Changing Attitudes

The American dream and the promise of opportunity brought many people to the United States. People who had no hope of owning land in Europe wanted to buy land in their new country. Others would practice their trades and earn a living.

Many were successful at achieving their dreams. However, many others faced devastating hardships. Some people were disabled or died from war, accidents, or disease. Some ethnic groups were met with discrimination and were unable to find work. Women with small children were sometimes widowed and unable to work. Poverty, exposure to freezing weather, malnutrition, and starvation were very real possibilities. Many people assumed that being poor meant a person had failed in some way. They thought poor people needed to work harder or make different choices in order to succeed.

Prior to World War I (1914–1918), more than half of U.S. citizens lived on farms or in rural areas. While there was rural poverty, people looked to extended families and members of the local communities for support. The people who migrated to the cities in search of work no longer had the support of nearby family and community.

Children of poor families were fed at the Children's Aid Society.

A new philosophy of welfare, called social work, emerged. Social work focused on helping individual poor people take advantage of the opportunities in the United States. Social workers counseled people to help them find ways out of poverty, and communities and religious groups continued their social services. But the federal government still believed such aid should be handled locally.

Mothers' Pensions

Lawmakers did agree that some people were clearly poor because of circumstance, such as widows and those who were physically or mentally unable to work. The government paid pensions to widows of Civil War soldiers and injured veterans. It also funded institutions for the mentally ill, although the living conditions remained substandard for decades.

After World War I and into the 1920s, the government created new programs to provide small amounts of money to widows with children. Legislators believed that women should not be in the workforce but at home with their children. Local governments handled the pension programs. These pensions were almost exclusively given to white women. Few African-American widows received any support. Most welfare programs excluded African Americans until the 1960s and the civil rights movement.

Pensions

The idea for Mothers' Pensions emerged because state officials were pulling children out of their homes and placing them in orphanages when their mothers were too poor to care for them. New York and Illinois were among the first states to try a different approach. Instead of taking children away, they started giving the mothers cash—the same amount that it would cost the state to house the children in an orphanage. In 1911, Illinois passed the first official Mothers' Pension law. Within five years, 26 other states had done the same.

Ellis Island Immigration Station in 1902

Chapter 4

Jobless and homeless men waited in line for a free dinner during the Great Depression.

Federal Welfare and Policy Changes

With the end of World War I, the U.S. economy grew during the 1920s. Many people made a lot of money. Some deposited their savings in banks. Others invested their earnings in the stock market. People who invested in the stock market hoped that the stocks they purchased would increase in value over time.

On October 24, 1929, the stock market crashed. The stocks had lost their value. Instead of becoming richer, investors suddenly became poorer. It was a frightening time. Banks failed and people lost their savings. Businesses also lost money, which made it difficult for them to pay their employees. People changed their spending habits, and businesses began laying people off.

The *Almanac of American History* reports that when the stock market crashed, the unemployment rate in the United States was approximately 3.2 percent. The economic situation worsened over the next five years with the Great Depression and the drought across the Midwest. More people lost their jobs. By 1933, the unemployment rate was almost 25 percent. The nation was desperate for relief.

The New Deal

Franklin Delano Roosevelt was elected president during the Great Depression. He took office on March 4, 1933. President Roosevelt understood that millions of unemployed workers and starving families across the United States needed help.

He believed it was the government's job to find a solution. President Roosevelt promised Americans that a New Deal was coming. He enlisted smart, creative people to help him develop ideas to improve the economy. These prominent scholars, law professors, and economists discussed solutions to the country's problems. This group became known as Roosevelt's Brain Trust.

President Roosevelt spent his first 100 days in office launching programs to help end the Depression and give people hope. He created the Public Works Administration to give people government jobs. The Civilian Conservation Corps put young men to work on projects in rural areas and national parks. The Agricultural Adjustment Act helped save failing farms. The Federal Housing Administration provided home

Works Progress Administration

After a few years, President Roosevelt shut down the Public Works Administration. He created a similar agency called the Works Progress Administration (WPA). This agency provided approximately 3 million people with jobs within a year. Some of the jobs involved physical labor, such as clearing wood from forests and building roads, bridges, schools, and power plants. The WPA also supported artistic projects by giving money to playwrights, mural painters, artists, and authors.

loans, and the Rural Electrification Administration installed electricity in rural areas. All these programs gave people much-needed jobs. They also responded to the needs of desperate farmers struggling through the Dust Bowl and businesses enduring in an uncertain economy.

The Social Security Act

Even with all these programs, and the passage of a minimum wage law, it took many years for the country to rise out of the Depression. More needed to be done. President Roosevelt signed the Social Security Act in 1935. This act provided unemployment stipends for laid-off workers, people with disabilities, widows, and the elderly. President Roosevelt created a new tax in order to pay for these programs. The new tax required all workers and employers to contribute to Social Security. President Roosevelt promised young workers that the money they paid into the program would be returned to them when they were old enough to receive Social Security benefits.

The Social Security Act also included a section to provide aid to dependent children. Most of the benefits went to Caucasian, single mothers. The law's

President Roosevelt warned that the government could not continue forever to carry the burden of unemployment.

purpose was to ensure that poor children would not go hungry. The Social Security legislation was not universally accepted. People worried that generous welfare would discourage people from working.

The Social Security Act formed the basis for laws that still exist. Social Security legislation has changed over the years, but the basic idea of the program remains the same. Lawmakers continue to debate and discuss the value of Social Security and the Aid to Dependent Children concept. These programs helped pull the nation out of the Great Depression.

A War Economy and the Cold War Era

In 1941, the United States entered World War II. The war helped the economy. New jobs opened in factories and the armed services. Women entered the workforce in great numbers to aid the war effort. The jobs created by the Works Progress Administration were no longer needed, so the agency closed.

When the war ended in 1945, people wanted to think about home and family, peace, and prosperity. Social Security and the Depression-era aid programs quietly continued.

The Cold War between the Union of Soviet Socialist Republics (USSR) and the United States began in the 1940s. The war was a competition between two ideas—the U.S. economic system of capitalism and the Soviet economic system of communism.

By the 1950s, the U.S. poverty rate reached 25 percent, but mainstream society avoided talking about welfare. Many U.S. citizens became afraid to talk about the gap between rich and poor. They feared they might sound like communists. But the silence did not last long.

Welfare Discrimination

Today, most people have their own impression of the "typical" welfare recipient. These generalizations may be based partly on truth and partly on stereotypes. Minorities and unmarried mothers are two of these groups. However, in the 1940s and 1950s, these now "typical" welfare recipients were often deliberately excluded. African-American families received far less aid than Caucasian families, despite desperate needs within minority communities.

The Aid to Dependent Children (ADC) program screened out "undesirable" Caucasian clients, too. They did not approve of unmarried women having children, so they refused to support them. Women who the caseworkers considered promiscuous were also excluded. ADC staff made surprise midnight house visits to make sure that homes were clean and free of boyfriends.

Politics

The 1960s and 1970s were a time of great political and social unrest. A country that had been united during World War II became politically divided over the war in Vietnam. U.S. students and pacifists protested against the nation's involvement in Vietnam, but many other people believed that the war was right.

African Americans began standing up for equal rights as citizens. Women pushed for gender equality in the workforce. Poor people wanted government-aid programs to assist them with their basic needs.

These divisions began to shape politics more and more. Even when the Democrats and Republicans could agree on an issue, they could not agree on what kind of policies would make the best changes. Many issues came up for debate—including welfare policies.

President Johnson signed the Civil Rights Act on July 2, 1964.

Great Society

In 1964, President Lyndon Baines Johnson gave a speech in which he declared his intention to make the United States of America into the Great Society. The goals of the Great Society included creating equal opportunities for poor people and minorities, providing better health care and education, and lifting people out of poverty. President Johnson launched numerous programs to do this. He created Head Start preschool programs for poor children and paid for new teachers to be sent to inner-city schools. He introduced the Food Stamp program to help poor families buy groceries.

Health Insurance

One of the major pieces of the Great Society legislation created Medicare and Medicaid. Health care is expensive. Medicare provides health insurance for elderly people. Medicaid provides health insurance for poor families who cannot afford it.

Wealthy and middle-class families usually pay a set amount of money, called a premium, every month (even when they are healthy) to a health insurance company. Often, an employee's company pays all or part of the premium. When an employee becomes sick, the insurance company pays all or a portion of the medical bills.

Poor families generally cannot afford to make these monthly payments. They may be unemployed. Or, they may work for a company that does not provide insurance or pay for a portion of its cost. When these people are sick, they must pay the full cost of a doctor's appointment or hospital visit out of their own pockets. Medical costs are so high that sometimes poor people must choose whether to stay sick or pay a doctor and possibly go without food. Elderly people tend to have more medical expenses. No longer working, they live on a limited budget.

Medicare and Medicaid programs helped a lot of people stay healthy and still have money to pay for food and housing. These programs still exist today.

War on Poverty

President Johnson declared an "unconditional war on poverty" when he talked about creating the Great Society. He started many programs designed to end poverty. The Economic Opportunity Act brought new businesses into poor communities

Great Society Legislation

Legislation passed during President Johnson's term includes:

- Civil Rights Act: prohibited discrimination due to race and sex
- Economic Opportunity Act: encouraged industries to move into struggling communities to create jobs and boost the economy
- Elementary and Secondary School Act: provided $1 billion for public schools and $100 million for library books and textbooks
- Food Stamp Act: gave poor families coupons to purchase groceries
- Higher Education Act: gave money to colleges for scholarships and tuition aid
- National Endowment for the Arts: supported arts programs and individual artists
- Omnibus Housing Act: gave $7.5 billion for low-income housing and urban renewal
- Voting Rights Act: ended literacy tests for voters and allowed monitoring of polls so people could not be turned away

to create jobs. Educational programs were launched to give people opportunities. The Higher Education Act provided scholarship money for colleges to admit more students who could not afford full tuition.

President Johnson also recognized that many of the country's poorest families were African Americans and had been mostly ignored in previous welfare policies. The Civil Rights Act of 1964 made race discrimination illegal. Employers could no longer refuse to hire qualified candidates because they were not Caucasian. African Americans began getting higher-paying jobs.

The political divide between liberals and conservatives grew particularly wide over the welfare debate as these policies emerged. Was the nation moving in the right direction? The questions lawmakers asked in the 1960s and 1970s are still being asked today.

"This administration, here and now, declares unconditional war on poverty in America. . . . It will not be a short or easy struggle, no single weapon of strategy will suffice, but we shall not rest until that war is won."[1]

—President Lyndon Baines Johnson, 1964

A Head Start class in Mississippi in April of 1966

Chapter 5

Former presidents Reagan, Carter, and Ford in 1991

1990s: New Welfare Reforms

The liberal policy initiatives launched under President Johnson's Great Society plan slowed from 1969 through 1992 as citizens elected a nearly uninterrupted series of conservative presidents. Richard Nixon, Gerald Ford, Ronald Reagan, and George H. W. Bush advocated for welfare laws that would minimize dependency. The Reagan administration (1981–1989), in particular, entered the White House at a time when citizens embraced his message of tax relief, personal responsibility, and a smaller federal government.

> "We should measure welfare's success by how many people leave welfare, not by how many are added."[1]
>
> —*President Ronald Reagan*

This brought new dimensions to the welfare debate. Previously, federal welfare policies had been liberal initiatives that conservatives pushed against. Reagan began by clearly expressing a conservative vision for welfare reform. This vision emphasized strengthening families by encouraging two-parent homes and increasing employment opportunities. Conservatives wanted states, instead of the federal government, to control welfare programs, and they wanted to end the dependency on welfare benefits.

Family Support Act

Near the end of Reagan's term in office, The Family Support Act of 1988 was signed. This act formalized some of the conservative recommendations. The bill required states to move 20 percent of their Aid to Families with Dependent Children recipients from welfare into jobs or training programs within three years. The bill also provided additional Medicaid and funding for child care that could help people's attendance and performance at work. This legislation was intended to end the entitlement-based system of welfare that had emerged in the 1960s. In an entitlement system, the recipients receive aid in cash and there are no time limits on how long they can receive the aid. For many, this provided no incentive to find employment. Conservative leaders wanted to be sure that poor people worked for their financial aid money, even if that money was paid in the form of welfare. The intent of welfare was to offer a second chance, not to become a way of life.

Clinton's Policy Recommendations

President Bill Clinton began his first term in 1993 with a plan to overhaul welfare. As governor of Arkansas, Clinton had been involved in developing the Family Support Act. President Clinton wanted to continue welfare-to-work programs and expand them. He supported two-year time limits on welfare and aggressive work requirements. Even among liberals, the concept of welfare without some responsibilities began to fade.

> "We have to make welfare what it was meant to be—a second chance, not a way of life. . . . let this be the year we end welfare as we know it."[2]
> —*President Bill Clinton, 1995 State of the Union address*

President Clinton strongly advocated for additional support measures that would help people keep jobs. These measures included extending Medicaid coverage, providing child care, and offering transportation vouchers. The goal was to make parents better able to succeed at a job without jeopardizing their children. Clinton spoke to issues that the Republicans (conservatives) wanted, such as time limits on welfare. He also addressed issues that Democrats (liberals) wanted, such as guarantees that after the time limit was over, poor people would not be abandoned. It appeared that Clinton might be able to bring people together to create a solution to welfare.

Turning Ideas into Law

In theory, the ideas of the Clinton administration seemed like a good compromise. In reality, it was difficult for liberals and conservatives to agree on how to turn the ideas into laws. Important questions arose. How long should the time limits be? Should the federal government decide which programs to offer, or should it give money to the states to decide what is best? What would happen to people who were still unemployed or struggling when their time limit on welfare ended?

Some conservatives wanted stronger limits on who could benefit from welfare. Speaker of the House Newt Gingrich suggested that the government refuse welfare to immigrants, teenage mothers, children born out of wedlock, and children born into families already receiving

Angry Democrats

President Clinton had promised the country welfare reform. And in order to make that happen, he was willing to make big compromises that his political party did not always agree with. Democrats who had supported President Clinton's stance on securing post-welfare solutions for the poor were upset when the president signed the Temporary Assistance for Needy Families (TANF) bill without these provisions. They believed that he had given up on a very important liberal value: providing long-term welfare support for those who need it most.

Welfare advocates believed Clinton gave in too soon to conservative pressure. Several leaders in the Democratic Party publicly criticized Clinton's decision. Senator Christopher Dodd called the bill "an unconscionable retreat from a 60-year commitment that Republicans and Democrats, 10 American presidents, and congresses have made on behalf of [America's] children."[3]

welfare money. He believed that if fewer people were eligible for welfare, fewer people would expect it, and the government could spend less money. He also thought the government had a responsibility not to reward people who, in his opinion, had made immoral choices.

Most liberals disagreed with Gingrich. They argued that people should not be punished for past behavior. They also felt strongly that if time limits became part of the law, so should some provisions for taking care of low-income people when their time limits expired. Liberals did not view welfare as a handout, but as necessary support to people making less money than they needed. Some liberals were concerned that time limits would increase poverty if former welfare recipients were not able to get better-paying jobs.

The Compromise: Approved Policy Changes

President Clinton agreed with liberals about the necessity of post-welfare solutions as a part of the new welfare law. Conservatives refused to support the law if it included those provisions. Eventually, President Clinton decided to support the law without these provisions. The nation needed welfare reform.

On August 22, 1996, President Clinton signed the Personal Responsibility and Work Opportunities Reconciliation Act (PRWORA). It created a new welfare program called Temporary Assistance for Needy Families (TANF). The law imposed time limits on welfare recipients, supported welfare-to-work programs, and required states to provide job training for welfare recipients. TANF replaced Aid to Families with Dependent Children. The federal government would give TANF money to states, which would then create specific programs to meet its goals. The TANF program was reauthorized in 2006 under President George W. Bush.

SCHIP

Some parents who work do not earn enough to pay the cost of private health coverage for their children, but they earn too much to qualify for Medicaid.

Programs to help the poor with the cost of health care were expanded under President Clinton. The State Children's Health Insurance Program (SCHIP) is designed to help low-income families who do not qualify for Medicaid. Welfare reforms allow people to receive medical care from Medicaid even if they work and after they stop receiving welfare.

President Clinton prepared to give his State of the Union address on January 24, 1995.

Chapter 6

In March 2005, U.S. Treasury Secretary John Snow (center) said the Medicaid program would be out of funds in 2020.

The Welfare Controversy Today

A vital question is at the center of the welfare controversy. What is the government's responsibility to its citizens? The Constitution promises each citizen the right to life, liberty, and the pursuit of happiness. U.S. citizens tend to believe that the government should protect both individual freedom and collective security. This means, among other things, that the government should protect each person's right to earn money and collect wealth. It also means that the government should protect vulnerable populations from injury and suffering. Is it possible to do both with limited financial resources?

Who Pays for Welfare?

Federal, state, and local governments collect taxes from citizens to pay for welfare programs. Taxes are an important part of the capitalist system. Taxes pay the salaries of government employees, such as members of Congress, police officers, and postal workers. Taxes pay for the armed forces and the construction of roads and bridges. They pay for agencies that monitor products such as medication, toys, cars, and meat to ensure consumer safety. Politicians and lawmakers spend much of their time deciding how much tax money the government should collect and how that money should be spent.

People pay taxes based on a percentage of their yearly income. People with high salaries pay more taxes than people with low salaries. People who receive welfare make so little money that they do not pay very much in taxes. This difference is a challenge for the welfare debate. When the government pays for roads and police officers, these services benefit everyone. When the government pays for welfare, it primarily benefits poor people. Is that fair to those who pay most of the taxes? Welfare supporters believe it is fair for the government to ask those who have money to support those who do not. Welfare opponents disagree.

Parental Employment

The National Center for Children in Poverty reports that the majority of children living in poverty have parents who work.

Welfare Goals: What Supporters Believe

Welfare supporters believe that government aid to poor people is the best, most direct way to end poverty. Welfare supporters are mainly concerned about ending the suffering of poor and struggling families. They favor programs that help unemployed people who struggle financially when they are in between jobs. They also favor programs that support people who have jobs but still do not earn enough to cover basic costs. Ideally, these programs would be easy to access and available to those who need them.

Welfare supporters use language carefully to convey their points. They talk about lifting people out of poverty, providing stepping-stones to success, and helping people get back on their feet. They promote equality, the leveling of the playing field for disadvantaged families, and protecting children from hunger and homelessness. Those who favor welfare accuse opponents of being heartless for placing the financial interests of wealthy people above the basic human needs of poor people. Supporters believe that the government has a moral obligation to keep people out of poverty by any means available.

How Money from Taxes Is Spent

The Center on Budget and Policy Priorities studies government policies and programs. In May 2007, it released a report explaining how federal tax money is spent. The major areas of government spending include:

- Defense and security: 21 percent. War in Iraq and Afghanistan, the Department of Defense, security-related services
- Social Security: 21 percent. Retirement benefits to retired workers, survivors' benefits, disability benefits
- Miscellaneous public services: 21 percent. Benefits to military veterans and retired federal employees, overseeing safe foods and drugs, and building roads, bridges, and airports
- Medicare, Medicaid, and the State Children's Health Insurance Program: 19 percent
- Safety net programs: 9 percent. Earned Income Tax Credit (EITC) refunds; food stamps, school lunches, housing aid
- National debt: 9 percent. Money owed by the U.S. Treasury

In 1918, labor leader Eugene V. Debs stated,

> *In this country . . . there are still vast numbers of our people who are the victims of poverty and whose lives are an unceasing struggle all the way from youth to old age. . . . It is due entirely to the outgrown social system in which we live.*[1]

Welfare Goals: What Opponents Believe

All welfare opponents are not necessarily against all forms of welfare. Some certainly are, but others are concerned about the welfare system and believe it could be drastically improved by limiting its scope. Welfare opponents are concerned that poor people will become dependent on welfare and unable to ever help themselves. They also worry that people who do not really need help will take advantage of the system if the government makes it too easy to receive aid. If welfare programs must exist, opponents believe that the goal should be to provide temporary aid that helps people as quickly as possible to get back on their feet and off welfare.

Welfare opponents also use language carefully. They talk about ending welfare dependency, stopping government handouts, and promoting self-sufficiency. They encourage personal responsibility and tax relief to reward hardworking citizens. They accuse supporters of wanting to create a welfare state in which people will become accustomed to handouts and not seek work. Welfare opponents believe that the government should not endlessly support people who, in their view, do not contribute enough financially to society.

In 1933, physician Francis Everett Townsend stated,

> *the citizenry must take charge of their government. . . . Taking care of people runs against the American grain—against the feeling that everyone ought to hustle for himself.*[2]

A Complicated Issue

These two sides of the welfare debate are not the only ways to think about welfare. Most people do not fall neatly on one side or the other. It is possible to list the reasons why people might oppose welfare, but not everyone who opposes welfare shares the same concerns. This is also true for welfare supporters. For example, many people who are in favor of welfare also worry about dependency.

In general, liberals would rather see people fed and housed, even if it means they may become dependent on welfare. They believe that helping people will make them better able to seek employment. In general, conservatives would rather promote employment and a strong work ethic, even if it means some people may go hungry for a while. They believe that struggling people may rely on temporary shelters and soup kitchens until their circumstances motivate them to find work.

How can these issues be solved if there are so many different opinions? That may be the most difficult question regarding the welfare debate. Many controversial issues have two very clear, opposing viewpoints. Welfare is not one of those issues.

Complexity can be a good thing. It means there is room for citizens and lawmakers to explore the issue. There may be a workable solution in between the two extremes that has yet to be recognized. The complexity of the debate also poses its own set of challenges. With so many possible solutions, it is difficult to narrow them down.

"There is nothing wrong with America that cannot be cured by what is right with America."[3]

—President Bill Clinton, first inaugural address, January 20, 1993

Welfare Rights Committee members hung a protest sign in Minnesota's state capitol on April 29, 2005.

Chapter 7

Howard Dean testified at Senate welfare hearings in 1995.

Key Questions in the Welfare Debate

No matter how much people debate whether the government should provide welfare, it does not change the fact that welfare programs currently exist. Most of the debate centers around how to reform the existing welfare programs to best serve the country. Welfare supporters want to see programs expanded. Welfare opponents want to see more limits placed on government spending. People not only have ideas about how to do that, but they also present questions that need answers. Who should be able to receive welfare and for how long? Should welfare recipients be required to work? Who should oversee the programs, and how can they be sure people are not abusing the system?

Eligibility

The major issue is determining who should be eligible for welfare. This dictates how much money the government will need to spend on welfare each year. If eligibility criteria are broad, welfare costs will be high and more people will be eligible to seek aid. If eligibility criteria are narrow, welfare costs will be low and many people will not meet the eligibility requirements.

Low income is the primary criterion for welfare eligibility. However, it is not a fixed criterion.

What Does *Poor* Really Mean?

The government must decide who is considered poor. Classifying people as having a low income is not easy. Some people believe that poverty should be measured strictly by calculating the amount of money needed for a family to buy what they need. If a family's income falls below that line, they should be called poor.

Other people believe that, in some cases, people above the line also should be considered poor. They believe the definition of poor should depend, in part, on the wealth of other people in the society.

Lawmakers regularly reconsider how low a family's income level must be to receive welfare. The income requirements may be different for cash assistance, food stamps, Medicaid, and other aid.

Welfare opponents have proposed many different types of eligibility limitations in addition to income. For instance, welfare programs could require people to participate in job training, prove they are looking for work, or attend counseling sessions. Many state-based welfare initiatives add these criteria.

Time Limits

Should there be a limit on how long a person can receive assistance? Most welfare opponents say yes. Most welfare supporters say no. The existing Temporary Assistance for Needy Families (TANF) grants, established in 1996 and renewed in 2006, place time limits on welfare checks for each family. A continuous three-year limit was set as well as a total five-year lifetime limit. Most families do not need welfare for more than two years. Poverty for most people is temporary.

Welfare opponents believe that time limits ensure that the system remains as a temporary fix for families who have fallen on hard times—not an endless handout program. Welfare supporters worry that some families would not have the ability to secure a sufficient income over such a short period of time.

Welfare Management

Should welfare be handled at the state or federal level? Chances are the needs of a poor family in New York might be different from the needs of a poor family in Iowa. Are those needs different enough that each state should serve its residents differently? Supporters of federal welfare say no. They believe that people all over the country have the same basic needs, so the federal government should have laws

Still Struggling

The government recognizes that even if a family is above the poverty threshold, the family may still be struggling. Many government programs base eligibility on different income guidelines. For example, some housing benefits are available to people whose income is above the amount specified as the poverty level. Programs that use the poverty guidelines this way include: Food Stamps, Low Income Home Energy Assistance Program, Head Start, and the National School Lunch Program.

Not all government-aid programs are based on the poverty guidelines. Programs such as TANF, the Earned Income Tax Credit, and low-rent public housing use different eligibility criteria. Social Security programs, such as Medicare, retirement benefits, and unemployment benefits, are entitlements and are not based on income.

that guarantee housing and food for all citizens. Supporters of state-based welfare say yes. They believe that welfare money will go further if the programs are tailored to meet the needs of fewer people in a state-based system.

The TANF grants are somewhat of a compromise between these two positions. The federal government collects money that it later returns to the states in the form of TANF block grants. The states can only use that money to pay for programs approved by TANF, but they can do it in the way that is best for their state's residents. The Administration for Children and Families reports that $16.5 billion in federal TANF funds were available in 2007.

Preventing Dependency

How do welfare programs balance the goals of alleviating poverty and minimizing welfare dependency? Welfare opponents believe that minimizing welfare dependency will lead to less poverty. Welfare supporters are not convinced that "dependency" is the right word to describe ongoing welfare support.

Does offering assistance encourage people to rely on welfare and not seek employment? Welfare

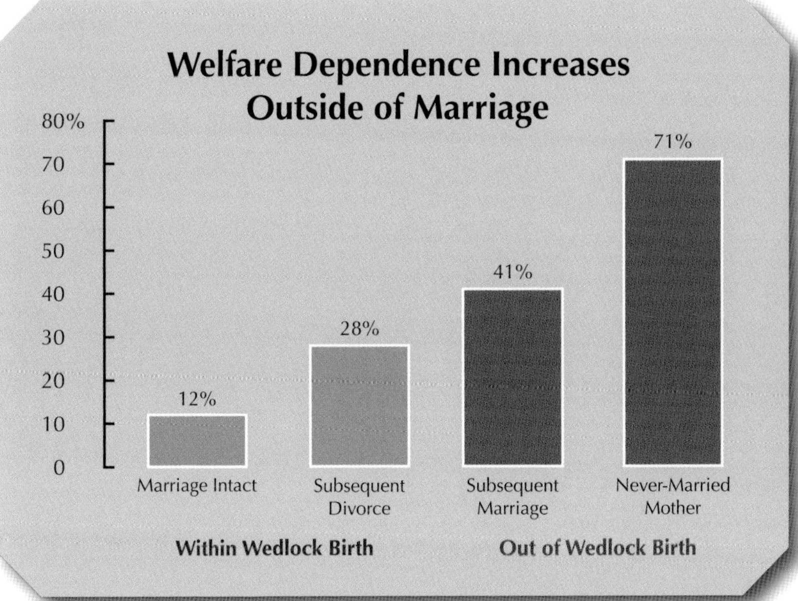

Marital status and welfare dependence based on a National Longitude Survey

programs are often structured so that recipients get money only when they do not have jobs. If they can only get a job that pays less than or equal to welfare, what is the incentive to work? And if welfare must be paid to supplement low-wage earnings, how will the need for those payments ever end?

Incentive Programs

One possibility for limiting dependency is to create incentive programs. These types of programs provide additional cash to welfare recipients for making certain decisions. Work incentives reward people on welfare who find employment. Marriage incentives reward families when unmarried parents get married. Often, two-income households do not qualify for welfare; therefore, fewer people remain in the system. Incentive programs are controversial. Do work incentives help people find jobs that work best for them? Should marriage be encouraged by the government? These issues continue to be debated.

Marriage Values Debate

Is keeping yourself off welfare a good reason to get married? Many conservatives say yes, because they believe marriage promotes healthy families and leads to long-term financial stability. Most liberals say no, because they believe that getting married just for financial reasons creates unhealthy families in the long run.

EITC

The Earned Income Tax Credit (EITC) is one of the biggest antipoverty programs. This program provides a federal supplement to working families with children who do not earn enough to lift them out of poverty. Unlike traditional welfare programs, a parent must work.

The more hours parents work, the more money they earn. The more they earn, the more money they receive from the government in the form of tax rebates. The less they work and earn, the less they receive in tax rebates. This program encourages people to work to receive help.

Welfare Abuse

How do you prevent people from taking advantage of the system? This issue concerns those who favor and those who oppose welfare. However, both welfare supporters and opponents have different ideas of what it means to abuse the welfare system. Welfare opponents are concerned that long-term welfare recipients take advantage of a "free ride." Welfare supporters claim that those long-term recipients face structural barriers to employment and financial independence.

Some welfare opponents suggest that large numbers of capable workers choose not to work in exchange for welfare money—while others are out working and earning the tax dollars to pay for that welfare. Welfare opponents often use this type of example to convey an image of welfare recipients as lazy freeloaders. Welfare supporters respond by saying that such a scenario rarely occurs. They claim that no one who could be earning more would choose welfare as an option, because the payments are so small. They counter that image by pointing to the historical legacies based on racism, sexism, and classism that have prevented poor people from climbing the social and economic ladder. ∽

Personal Responsibility

Many conservatives believe that if welfare is too available, poor people will take extreme measures (such as having more children) in order to receive more welfare money. Newt Gingrich, former Speaker of the U.S. House of Representatives, believed in limiting welfare eligibility and benefits to two years.

In the early 1990s, Gingrich pushed for welfare reform. He opposed welfare payments to teen parents and unmarried mothers. Unwed mothers under the age of 18 would not receive welfare payments in cash. His policy plan would have denied additional welfare money for children born to a woman already on welfare. He believed that if people knew they could not obtain welfare for children born out of wedlock, single people would stop having babies.

This mother found she was better off financially when she was unemployed and on food stamps than working at minimum wage.

Chapter 8

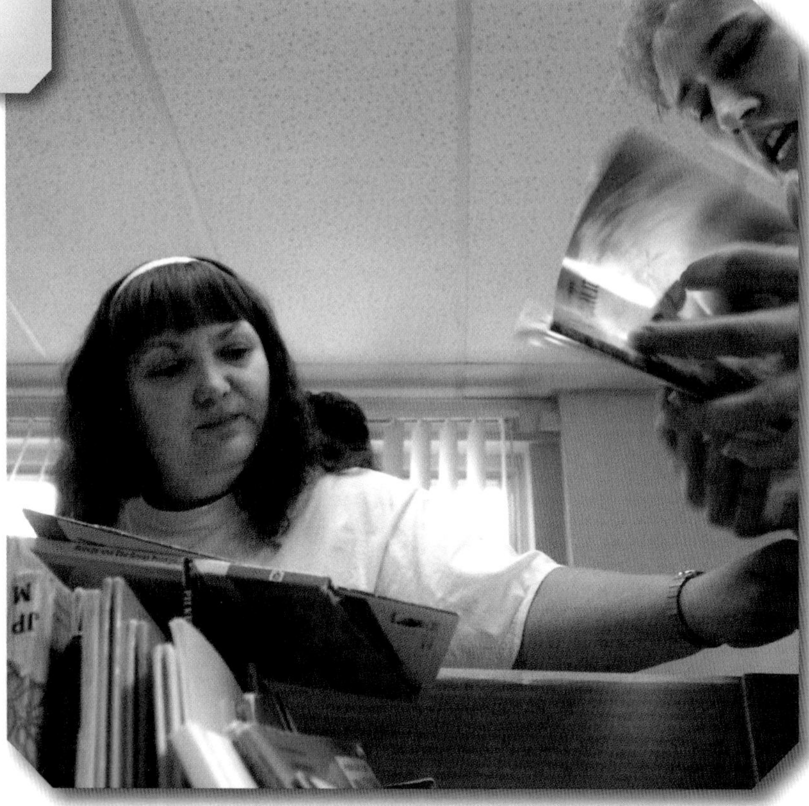

Geneva Goodson (left) *was on food stamps while she studied for her high school equivalency diploma.*

Welfare Strategies

The government has tried many different welfare strategies. Each plan has its benefits and its drawbacks as well as its supporters and its critics. Most of the plans require the government to spend money. The issue is determining where and how that money should be used. Should the money go to social workers to distribute as they consider appropriate? Should the money be used for job training programs or to support incentive programs? Should aid be received in the form of vouchers such as food stamps? Should financial support be distributed in such a way that it can be used for rent, housing, clothing, and items that were not intended to be part of welfare support?

Income Support: Cash in Hand

The most basic form of welfare occurs when the government gives poor families money to help with expenses. Many welfare supporters believe this is the best system to keep people out of poverty. Cash support can enable low-wage workers to live more comfortably. It provides income to unemployed people and prevents them from being hungry and homeless. Critics of income support worry that making "free" money available discourages people from getting and keeping jobs. They would rather pay for soup kitchens and homeless shelters for temporary

National School Lunch Program

One of the most successful welfare initiatives has been the National School Lunch Program that was established in 1946 by President Harry Truman. Children from low-income families who attend public school are provided with a free or reduced-cost school lunch. Some schools also offer breakfast programs. This program serves a group that everyone agrees deserves support: poor children.

use than permanent income support to keep poor people in homes. They believe this will motivate people to work.

Child Support: Making Both Parents Pay

The federal government showed a commitment to taking care of children by providing Mothers' Pensions in the 1920s and by passing the 1935 Aid to Dependent Children legislation. Much of this child support went to widows. In later years, the government recognized that more and more single mothers were not only widows but women who

Child Support Issues

Child support sometimes causes a problem even for middle-class families. If both parents are financially involved in a child's life, then both parents usually have physical custody or visitation rights. What happens if one parent feels the child is not safe with the other parent?

There is no clear solution. If refusing money from one parent places the other parent on welfare, what should the government require families to do? There are two apparent options. One option is to enter into a child support arrangement that may put the child at risk. The second option is to become part of the government's welfare system for support. There are people who feel strongly about each option. Which is more important: a parent's freedom to choose who their child spends time with or a family's financial independence? How should the second parent's fitness as a caretaker be evaluated? Would this decision be made by the parents, the family court judges, or the welfare system? Are there other possible solutions?

were divorced or had never married their children's fathers. Those fathers were earning incomes. States began creating child support laws that required both parents to financially support their children, even if the children lived with only one parent.

This plan held good news for both sides of the debate. Child support laws helped keep many single parents from needing welfare. It also helped the government spend less on cash support to families with children. However, there is a downside to child support laws. If one parent fails to pay, the other parent may not be eligible for government welfare to make up for the difference. The custodial parent is dependent on the child support money, whether or not it is paid.

Voucher Programs: Controlling Spending

Some people prefer the idea of vouchers as opposed to straight cash assistance. Food stamps, energy assistance, and housing vouchers allow the government to support the poorest families but still control how the money is spent. These programs often appeal to welfare supporters who worry about the pitfalls of cash support and welfare critics who want to help those most in need while lawmakers seek a better long-term solution. Critics of voucher programs believe that people may become dependent on the vouchers and not be motivated to change their lives on their own.

Job Training: The Benefits of Work

Most people involved in the welfare debate agree that it would be ideal if everyone who is capable of working could have a job. For many reasons, this has never been the case. There are always some people who are unemployed, whether for a short time or a long time.

One welfare program idea is job training. The government provides classes for people who have minimal education or who have trouble keeping a job. These classes might help people learn to read, learn a particular skill, or learn about a type of business. A person who completes the class will be better qualified to find a job. Those jobs pay slightly more than minimum wage. By learning skills to work at higher paying jobs, people could get themselves out of poverty. This concept is ideal to welfare opponents; supporters worry that job training is not enough.

Social Work: The Individual Approach

Many cash welfare recipients are required to participate in work programs. For some, this means programs related to job readiness. It also can address issues such as on-the-job training or vocational training. For others, it means helping individuals and families facing problems such as domestic violence or substance abuse. The goal of work programs is to help individuals work through the system to improve their position.

People on both sides of the welfare debate see value in work programs. However, they do not always agree on who should pay for them. Welfare supporters want tax money to support work program efforts. Welfare critics believe that privately funded organizations would be better equipped to handle this.

Incentives: A Reason to Change?

In the 1980s and 1990s a new approach to welfare emerged. Welfare critics suggested that incentives be developed. These would encourage welfare families to take actions that would ultimately result in their no longer needing government aid. One example is a work incentive that rewards people who keep jobs by giving them higher amounts of cash support or other benefits. However, for a woman on the Aid to Families with Dependent Children (formerly Aid to Dependent Children) program, her payment was reduced by a dollar for every dollar she earned. This became an incentive not to work.

Marriage benefits are another incentive. The majority of people who receive welfare are single parents, especially single mothers. Marriage incentives are the government's promise to give single mothers more welfare money each month if they get married, ideally to the father of their children. These incentives are based on the belief that marriage leads to strong families, which leads to financial stability.

But the debate over marriage incentives is heated. Most welfare supporters do not favor the idea and argue that the institution of marriage should not be used as a bargaining chip. They believe incentives could lead people into marriage just to

Deadbeat Dads

The phrase "deadbeat dads" was used by conservatives in the 1980s to describe fathers who were not financially involved in raising their children. Liberals argued it was not fair to threaten poor fathers with jail time for not paying child support when they legitimately could not afford it. Rather than spend public resources on urging these men to pay child support, liberals pressed for job training programs that allowed men to get jobs that helped them to meet their child support responsibilities.

Florida Governor Jeb Bush described legislation to get deadbeat dads to pay their child support in 2005.

receive extra money. If the family later becomes financially stable and no longer eligible for welfare support, what will happen to the marriage? Critics believe if a marriage is urged by government, and is not a result of love, it is doomed to fail.

Welfare opponents often approve of marriage incentives. Because two-parent families are more likely to thrive, they believe that these incentives will help people become self-sufficient. Otherwise, a couple might remain unmarried in order for one of them to collect welfare checks.

Tax Relief: Trust the Market to Provide

Some welfare critics argue that some form of government aid to the poor is needed, but they believe the current systems are flawed. Other welfare critics consider the welfare system to be hopelessly flawed and believe it cannot be mended. The strongest welfare opponents believe the government should end welfare altogether.

Many taxpayers argue that they should not continue paying for a system that has failed. If business owners could keep that tax money, they would be a little bit better off and could afford to pay their employees more. If salaries increase, people could get out of poverty on their own. These welfare opponents believe that the government should trust businesses to take care of their employees. This argument frustrates welfare supporters who fear that business owners would not raise salaries, but keep the profits. Welfare supporters contend that lowering taxes and eliminating welfare would only increase the divide between rich and poor.

President Bush met with community members after speaking about welfare reform at a Washington DC church.

Chapter 9

A January 10, 2007, news conference to discuss a bill to increase the minimum wage

Challenges to Resolving the Debate

The welfare debate in the United States is complex. Even those whose job it is to study welfare programs do not always agree on the best approach. Why is it so difficult to resolve the issues?

Social Attitudes toward Poor People

What causes poverty? There is no simple answer. When people cannot agree on the causes, it is difficult to agree on whether poor people deserve help.

Welfare supporters believe that the country's economic structure leads some people to poverty. Thus, poverty is not the fault of poor people, and the government should help them. Welfare opponents believe that individuals' choices lead them to poverty. Thus, people who end up poor are at least partly responsible for their situation, and the government should not be obligated to help. These are only the most extreme positions. Some people believe poverty is caused by a combination of the two extremes.

The lack of a clear reason for the cause of poverty makes the welfare debate difficult. Is welfare a right? Is it something people deserve regardless of the choices they make? Should children suffer for

Privatization

Some people believe that welfare should be handled only by private organizations. They argue that nonprofit organizations can raise money from voluntary supporters instead of unwilling taxpayers. They believe that this approach might encourage donors to give higher amounts because the donations are tax deductible. It would also reduce federal government control and allow communities to create local solutions that best serve the people of their area.

their parents' inability to support them? Welfare supporters believe that even asking these questions leads people to feel prejudiced against poor people. It suggests that lawmakers should try to judge a person's intentions and efforts to see if they are worthy of aid. How can those things be judged?

Economics

Welfare programs are always connected to conversations about the economy. Different people have different ideas about what strategies will keep the economy working best. It all comes back to the American dream. Over time, U.S. citizens have come to believe that financial success is possible for everyone. But is it really possible for everyone?

Strong opponents of welfare say yes, opportunities are out there. People just need to take advantage of them. Those who find jobs or learn new skills often can earn enough to get out of poverty. If people cannot improve their own circumstances,

Bootstraps

The phrase "pulling yourself up by your bootstraps" means doing something yourself or overcoming a challenge without any outside help.

A bootstrap is a piece of leather or cloth sewn like a handle onto boots to make them easier to pull on. Actually lifting yourself by your own bootstraps is really quite difficult, probably impossible, but that is part of what makes the idiom meaningful. Those who struggle for financial success must work really hard, and, for many, it will be impossible.

there is something wrong. Alternatively, strong supporters of welfare say no, financial success is not possible for everyone even when poverty is often a temporary condition. For some, breaking the alternating cycles of poverty and employment is a constant struggle in their lives. The jobs that pay minimum wage will still exist. People will need to work those jobs. That means there will always be some poor and some rich people.

Goal Setting

Another challenge is that people cannot agree on what success means. Does success mean having fewer people on welfare? Does it mean more families living above the poverty threshold? Does it mean less government intervention and

Determining Success

Lawmakers face challenges when the goals of a welfare project are not clear. They are further challenged when statistics can be used in different ways. Does the money spent on welfare reduce poverty? Or does the money spent on welfare increase dependency?

For example, in 1986, President Reagan commented on welfare. He stated that as a result of former President Johnson's war on poverty, "Poverty, as measured by dependency, stopped shrinking and actually began to grow worse."[1] Though Reagan did not quote numbers, the words he chose indicated his perspective. He was measuring poverty based on the number of people still taking welfare money. He saw that increase as a failure.

A welfare supporter might view that same increase as a success, because it meant there were fewer families in poverty.

spending? Does it mean more people are employed? Each of these goals would require a special approach to welfare. When the people who must work together to create welfare programs have different goals in mind, it is difficult to create a single plan that can succeed in reaching any of the goals.

Using Statistics

Statistics are not always trustworthy, even though they are based on facts and research. Much depends on how the numbers are presented and interpreted. People who disagree often use identical statistics to support very opposite points of view.

Statistics can be misleading. For example, according to the 2006 census, 7.7 million families were considered to be living below the poverty threshold. However, some of those families received welfare money that moved their income above the poverty threshold. Welfare supporters could present the statistic based on the family's income without welfare to demonstrate the continued need for welfare. Welfare opponents could present the statistic based on the family's income including welfare. Demonstrating fewer families in poverty would help justify cutting welfare spending.

Other Issues Affecting Welfare

It is difficult for lawmakers to think effectively about welfare policies without considering some other issues. For instance, laws about housing, health care, education, and immigration all impact welfare recipients.

Housing is usually the largest monthly expense for most families. Poor families often must use more than half of their income on rent. This leaves little for utilities, food, clothing, and other needs. Housing policies can help save money. When housing policies change, it affects many people who receive welfare.

Health care is another major expense for families. Medicaid helps some poor families, but does the program cover all the people who need it? The question of who should be eligible for Medicaid impacts the welfare debate. Welfare supporters believe if the government provides people with free or inexpensive health care, it will help keep sick people from ending up on welfare. Welfare opponents see Medicaid as a form of welfare, and some believe that expanding the program would not be a good use of government money.

Education has been called the great equalizer because learning helps a person achieve success. Any student, whether rich or poor, can do well in school, but most people need support in order to do their best. Poor families tend to have less access to good books, computers, and the Internet, all of which help students learn. Schools in poor neighborhoods often struggle to provide enough materials for their students. Many people believe that this is not fair.

If students from poor families cannot get a good education, how will they compete with students from wealthier families for jobs and acceptance to college? How can they climb out of poverty if being poor prevents them from getting the skills to do so? Many welfare supporters believe that better education policies could help poor children break the poverty cycle. An education and a good job could keep them from needing welfare when they grow up.

Immigration laws also impact how welfare can benefit some of the nation's poorest people. Undocumented immigrants often work jobs that pay less than minimum wage. But they still must live, find housing, buy food, and use the health care system.

A May 7, 1997, rally protested a new welfare law that affected immigrants.

Chapter 10

Parents Barry and Maria Prince received Women, Infants, and Children (WIC) benefits.

Moving Forward

Lawmakers continue to struggle with the welfare debate. In the meantime, they must develop and maintain programs to fulfill the current welfare laws. The federal government offers more than 70 poverty-based welfare programs. The programs are administered by various departments of the federal government. The departments include: Agriculture, Education, Health and Human Services, Housing and Urban Development (HUD), Labor, and Treasury. The agencies within these departments cooperate with each other to provide services to people in need.

TANF

Temporary Assistance for Needy Families (TANF) funds are overseen by the Department of Health and Human Services. The rules placed on TANF grants to states have forced states to create programs that help people get and keep jobs.

In the last decade, TANF programs have highlighted the tension between the goals of getting people off welfare and getting people into good jobs. The government has learned that people who leave welfare when their time limit ends still look for support.

Most states continue job training, support, and career development programs for former welfare recipients to help them keep their jobs after the welfare money has run out. The intent is that these programs will help former welfare recipients gain skills to advance into jobs that pay more than minimum wage. States are still looking for the best programs to do this. It is an ongoing struggle.

WIC

One focus of government welfare programs is to ensure that children living in poverty are taken care of. Welfare supporters and welfare opponents disagree on how well the existing plans are meeting that goal. The Women, Infants, and Children (WIC) program supports food programs, nutrition education, and health care for pregnant women, babies, and young children. This program is administered by the Food and Nutrition Service of the Department of Agriculture.

Farm Subsidies

The Department of Agriculture provides farm subsidies, or payments, to support struggling farmers. Some subsidies are offered to farmers so that they can sell crops at a lower cost to buyers but still make enough profit to cover their living expenses. These subsidies are controversial because some people believe the law is skewed to allow large corporate farms to receive big payments, while smaller independent family farms receive very little.

Other subsidies are given to prevent too much of one crop from flooding the market. A farmer might be paid to not grow a certain crop because the government fears there will be too much of it for sale that year and lower the price for everyone. Some people believe such subsidies unfairly reward farmers for not working.

Every five years, Congress must vote to reauthorize these subsidies as part of a farm bill. Farm subsidies are one way that Congress tries to address rural poverty.

Farm Support

According to the Roosevelt Institute, between 2003 and 2005, the federal government spent $50 billion on farm subsidies.

Wages and Tax Relief

The debates about changing minimum wage and tax rates continue. When the minimum wage increase came before Congress in 2007 for a vote, conservatives wanted to add a small-business tax cut at the same time. The bill ultimately passed without the tax cut, but the discussion about wage increases versus tax cuts continues.

Conservatives mention the trickle-down effect. This concept suggests that if businesses are allowed to keep more money before taxes, the extra money will trickle down to their employees and make a positive impact on the economy. This would also help those with lower incomes. Liberals do not believe the trickle-down effect actually works. They push for required higher wages in order to benefit low-income people directly.

Minimum Wage

The *Washington Post* reported that the 2007 minimum wage increase raised the incomes of 13 million people: 5.6 million who were earning minimum wage, plus 7.4 million who were already earning just a little more than the former minimum wage.

Future Conversation

The welfare debate has lessened, at least as far as widespread public conversation is concerned. Political candidates, however, must still position themselves on welfare issues. Their opinions have some effect on how people vote. However, it is no longer one of the most talked-about issues.

While government policies have changed, the core problem remains the same. The nation is populated with some rich people, some middle-class people, and some poor people.

What are their responsibilities to each other? How much should the government direct those responsibilities?

Millions of people living in poverty now benefit from government welfare programs. Many others do not qualify but wish they had some help. Should they get it?

Millions of wealthy and middle-class citizens pay taxes each year that support welfare programs. Some of them wish they did not have to pay so much. Should they have to? Others wish the government would ask for more. Should it?

People from all walks of life are still discussing these issues. Rich people, middle-class people, poor

How Poor Are the Poor?

People perceive poverty in different ways. This challenge for the debate comes back to whether people should be considered poor based on their material wealth or their wealth as compared to others around them. For instance, according to Robert Rector of the Heritage Foundation:

> *But only a small number of the 37 million persons classified as "poor" by the Census Bureau fit that description. While real material hardship certainly does occur, it is limited in scope and severity. Most of America's "poor" live in material conditions that would be judged as comfortable or well-off just a few generations ago. Today, the expenditures per person of the lowest-income one-fifth (or quintile) of households equal those of the median American household in the early 1970s, after adjusting for inflation.*[1]

people, workers, employers, scientists, statisticians, historians, lobbyists, and lawmakers all have ideas and knowledge to contribute to the welfare debate. When people care enough to debate and argue about their beliefs, it is a positive sign of a healthy democracy. This means that people want to take action.

The U.S. Capitol in Washington DC houses the legislative branch of the federal government.

Timeline

1601	1911	1929
Elizabethan Poor Laws are created in Britain.	Illinois is the first state to pass Mothers' Pension legislation to support widows with children.	The stock market crashes on October 24.

1941	1943	1962
The United States enters World War II.	The WPA has created as many as 8 million jobs. It closes as jobs increase due to World War II.	Aid to Dependent Children program is renamed Aid to Families with Dependent Children.

1933

President Roosevelt is inaugurated on March 4. He creates public welfare programs throughout his presidency.

1935

In April, President Roosevelt creates the Works Progress Administration (WPA) to create jobs and help the economy.

1935

The Social Security Act passes on August 14. It includes Aid to Dependent Children legislation.

1964

President Johnson declares a War on Poverty in his State of the Union address on January 8.

1964

President Johnson introduces the Great Society goals in a speech at the University of Michigan on May 22.

1964

The Civil Rights Act passes on July 2. It prohibits discrimination based on race and gender.

Timeline

1964

The Economic Opportunity Act passes on August 20.

1981

President Reagan is inaugurated on January 20. He promises tax cuts for the middle class and an end to handouts.

1996

President Clinton signs the Personal Responsibility and Work Opportunity Reconciliation Act (PRWORA) on August 22.

1997

Temporary Assistance for Needy Families (TANF) legislation is implemented on July 1.

1988

President Reagan signs the Family Support Act on October 13.

1995

In his State of the Union address on January 24, President Clinton promises to "end welfare as we know it."

2006

TANF legislation is reauthorized by President George W. Bush on February 8.

2007

On January 10, Congress votes to increase the minimum wage from $5.15 to $7.25 in stages over two years.

Essential Facts

At Issue

In Favor

- Unemployed and low-wage workers are not solely responsible for their situation and deserve public support so they can survive.
- Long-term welfare support can enable low-wage workers to live above the poverty threshold.
- It is right for taxes taken from wealthier people to support those who are unemployed and live on a low income.

Opposed

- Unemployed and low-wage workers need to take more responsibility for earning their own money.
- Long-term welfare recipients may become dependent on aid.
- It is unfair that taxes from working people are used to support those who are unemployed or have a low income.

Critical Dates

1933–1935

As part of President Roosevelt's New Deal, he promised U.S. citizens relief during the Great Depression. Programs and acts included the Civilian Conservation Corps, Public Works Administration, Securities and Exchange Commission, Rural Electrification Administration, Social Security Act, and Food Stamp Act.

1964–1965

As part of President Johnson's Great Society, legislation was passed to improve the lives of the poor and minorities. Initiatives designed to end poverty and promote equality included the Civil Rights Act, Economic Opportunity Act, Higher Education Act, Medicare, and Medicaid.

August 22, 1996

President Clinton signed the Personal Responsibility and Work Opportunities Reconciliation Act (PRWORA). This plan changed the welfare system. Recipients were required to work to receive assistance for a temporary period of time. Aid to Families with Dependent Children (AFDC) was replaced by Temporary Assistance for Needy Families (TANF). States would use federal TANF grants to create specific programs.

February 8, 2006

The TANF program was reauthorized under President Bush.

Quotes

"We have to make welfare what it was meant to be—a second chance, not a way of life." *—President William Clinton, 1995 State of the Union address*

"Taking care of people runs against the American grain—against the feeling that everyone ought to hustle for himself."
—Francis Everett Townsend, 1933

Additional Resources

Select Bibliography

Agel, Jerome B. *We, the People: Great Documents of the American Nation.* New York: Barnes & Noble, 1997.

Miller, James, and John Thompson. *Almanac of American History*. Washington, DC: National Geographic, 2006.

Schorr, Lisbeth B. with Daniel Schorr. *Within Our Reach: Breaking the Cycle of Disadvantage.* New York: Doubleday, 1988.

Shaw, Greg M. *The Welfare Debate*. Westport, CT: Greenwood Press, 2007.

Further Reading

Bausum, Ann. *Our Country's Presidents.* Washington, DC: National Geographic, 2005.

De Koster, Katie, Ed. *Poverty: Opposing Viewpoints.* San Diego, CA: Gale Group, 1994.

Hakim, Joy. *All the People.* New York: Oxford University Press, 1995.

Shebar, Sharon. *Franklin D. Roosevelt and the New Deal.* Hauppauge, NY: Barron's, 1987.

Web Links

To learn more about the welfare debate, visit ABDO Publishing Company on the World Wide Web at **www.abdopublishing.com**. Web sites about the welfare debate are featured on our Book Links page. These links are routinely monitored and updated to provide the most current information available.

For More Information

For more information on this subject, contact or visit the following organizations.

Franklin D. Roosevelt Presidential Library and Museum
4079 Albany Post Road, Hyde Park, NY 12538
800-FDR-VISIT
www.fdrlibrary.marist.edu/
The museum contains artifacts from Roosevelt's four terms as president, including exhibits on the New Deal, the first Hundred Days, the Social Security Act, and World War II.

Lyndon Baines Johnson Library and Museum
2313 Red River Street, Austin, TX 78705
512-721-0200
www.lbjlib.utexas.edu
The museum contains artifacts from Johnson's presidency, including a replica of the Oval Office as it appeared during his time in the White House. Traveling exhibits on American history are also displayed.

The United States Capitol
Washington, DC
202-225-6827
www.aoc.gov/cc/visit/index.cfm
Take a guided tour of this center of the legislative branch. Learn how laws are made, and see where members of Congress work. For tickets, visit the Capitol Guide Service Kiosk near the intersection of First Street Southwest and Independence Avenue.

Glossary

capitalism

An economic system based on individual wealth, private ownership of property, a free market, and government regulations.

census

A regular, official count of all the people in a country.

communism

An economic system based on shared wealth, public ownership of property, and a government-controlled market.

conservative

A person who believes in smaller government, or less legislation, usually a Republican.

criterion

A factor that helps in making a decision.

dependency

Relying on something in order to survive.

entitlement

The belief that a person deserves a particular benefit or reward.

incentive

A reward promised to someone in order to get them to do something.

liberal

A person who believes in bigger government, or more legislation, usually a Democrat.

lobbyist

A person whose job is to convince lawmakers to vote for certain laws.

Medicaid

A health recovery program administered by the states for those with low incomes or very high medical bills.

Medicare
A federal health insurance for those 65 and older as well as some people under 65 with certain disabilities or health conditions.

partisan
Taking sides.

pension
A sum of money paid regularly to a person based on certain conditions.

poorhouse
A place to house needy or dependent people at public expense.

poverty threshold
The amount of income below which a person is considered to be living in poverty.

reform
To fix or change.

shelter
A temporary residence provided for people without homes.

stipend
A small amount of money paid to someone in exchange for something.

tax rate
Determines the portion of a person's income that is paid to the government.

vouchers
Coupons with a designated dollar amount that can be exchanged for specified items, such as food.

welfare
Government programs that provide money and other kinds of assistance to poor families.

Source Notes

Chapter 1. Why Welfare?

1. Thomas Corbett. "Informing the Welfare Debate: Perspectives on Transforming Social Policy." Institute for Research on Poverty. Apr. 1997. 18 Feb. 2008 <http://www.irp.wisc.edu/research/welreform/national/informingwd.htm>.

Chapter 2. Key Players in the Welfare Debate

None.

Chapter 3. Origins of Welfare in the United States

None.

Chapter 4. Federal Welfare and Policy Changes

1. Lyndon Baines Johnson. "First State of the Union Address." American Rhetoric. 8 Jan. 1964. 18 Feb. 2008 <http://www.historicaldocuments.com/GreatSocietyLyndonJohnson.htm>.

Chapter 5. 1990s: New Welfare Reforms

1. Ronald Reagan. *ThinkExist.com Quotations*. 23 May 2008 <http://thinkexist.com/search/searchquotation.asp?search=welfare&q=author%3A%22Ronald+Reagan%22>.
2. William Jefferson Clinton. "State of the Union Address." 24 Jan. 1995. 12 Feb. 2008 <http://www.movingimage.us/cg96/1995sotu.htm>.
3. Greg M. Shaw. *The Welfare Debate.* Westport, CT: Greenwood Press, 2007. 129.

Chapter 6. The Welfare Controversy Today

1. Jerome B. Agel. *We, the People: Great Documents of the American Nation.* New York: Barnes & Noble, 1997. 506.
2. Ibid. 160.
3. Ann Bausum. *Our Country's Presidents.* Washington, DC: National Geographic, 2005. 189.

Chapter 7. Key Questions in the Welfare Debate
None.

Chapter 8. Welfare Strategies
None.

Chapter 9. Challenges to Resolving the Debate
1. Greg M. Shaw. *The Welfare Debate.* Westport, CT: Greenwood Press, 2007. 117.

Chapter 10. Moving Forward
1. Robert E. Rector. "How Poor Are America's Poor? Examining the 'Plague of Poverty' in America." The Heritage Foundation. 27 Aug. 2007 <http://www.heritage.org/Research/Welfare/bg2064.cfm>.

Index

Index Continued

About the Author

Kekla Magoon has a Master of Fine Arts in Writing for Children and Young Adults from Vermont College. Her work includes many different kinds of writing, but she especially enjoys writing historical fiction and nonfiction. When she is not writing books for children, she works with nonprofit organizations and helps with fund-raising for youth programs.

Photo Credits

Jack Star/PhotoLink, cover; Amy E. Powers/AP Images, 6; Jim Cole/AP Images, 11; Kelly McCall/AP Images, 15; Carolyn Kaster/AP Images, 16; Jason Reed/Reuters/Corbis, 21; North Wind Picture Archives, 22, 29; Bettmann/Corbis, 31; AP Images, 32, 36, 39; Charles Kelly/AP Images, 43; Craig Fujii/AP Images, 44; Ron Edmonds/AP Images, 51; Charles Dharapak/AP Images, 52; Tom Olmscheid/AP Images, 59; John Duricka/AP Images, 60; Ryan Haugen, 65; Brian McDermott/AP Images, 69; Jon C. Hancock/AP Images, 70; Steve Cannon/AP Images, 77; Luke Frazza/AFP/Getty Images, 79; Pablo Martinez Monsivais/AP Images, 80; Susan Walsh/AP Images, 87; Jacqueline Malonson/AP Images, 88; J. Scott Applewhite/AP Images, 95